Isaías vs. Ecuador
Justice Served

United Nations:
Isaias Human Rights
were violated by
Ecuadorian Government

UN Human Rights Committee
in the case of Communication No. 2244/2013

ZE | ZAVALA
EGAS
ACADEMIC DIVISION

Second Edition
© Jorge Zavala Egas, 2016

All rights reserved

ISBN: 978-1537145662

LIBRARY OF CONGRESS CATALOGING-IN-PUBLICATION-DATA

First edition. Ecuador.
© Jorge Zavala Egas, 2016

All rights reserved

Design by: www.alexlib.com

This book may not be reproduced in whole or in part or transmitted through any electronic or mechanical procedure, including photocopying, magnetic recording, or any information storage and retrieval system, without the author's express permission.

Table of Contents

Preamble 5

Opinion of the U.N. Human Rights
Committee in the case of
Communication No. 2244/2013 7

Appendix: Individual opinion (partly
dissenting) by Yuval Shany,
Committee member 37

Explanation of the Opinion of the
U.S. Human Rights Committee in
the case of Communication No.
2244/2013 39

Preamble

Roberto and William Isaías are proud members the third generation of Ecuadorian Isaíases. Since 1912 when their grandfather Emilio Isaias left Lebanon at the age of 19 and established in Ecuador, his descendants have remained true to their core Lebanese values: hard work, vision, and the capacity to adapt to changing situations. These hardworking entrepreneurs have continued to grow their family businesses, initially in the textile industry and subsequently expanding to the industrial, telecommunications, commercial, agricultural, and mining sectors.

For over eight years now, they and their families have been the victims of the fierce political persecution unleashed against them by President Rafael Correa. In an all-out effort to seize the leading television channels, media outlets, and prosperous companies owned by the Isaias family, the Ecuadorian president has brazenly manipulated the judicial and executive branches of the government. As part of this relentless and systematic persecution, the law has been retroactively applied, due process has been violated, the right to a defense has been effectively thwarted, guilt rather than innocence has been presumed, judgments have been issued unsupported by evidence, and the right to appeal has been denied, thereby rendering the Isaíses helpless at law.

The U.N. Human Rights Committee ruled in favor of the Isaias on June 2016; it affirmed that Roberto and William Isaías's human rights were violated and that their right to appeal and have a due process was blatantly ignored.

The Committee has ordered the government of Ecuador to make whole their rights and to return all of the family's seized assets.

Jorge Zavala Egas

United Nations  CCPR/C/116/D/2244/2013

International Covenant on Civil and Political Rights

Advance unedited version

General Distr.
June 3, 2016¶

Original: Spanish

Human Rights Committee

OPINION ADOPTED BY THE COMMITTEE UNDER ARTICLE 5(4) OF THE OPTIONAL PROTOCOL WITH RESPECT TO COMMUNICATION No. 2244/2013[*][**]

Submitted by: Roberto Isaías Dassum and William Isaías Dassum (represented by attorneys Xavier Castro Muñoz and Heidi Laniado Hollihan)

Alleged victim: The authors

State party: Ecuador

Date of communication: March 12, 2012 (initial submission)

References: Decision adopted in accordance with Article 97 of the Committee Regulations, transmitted to the State Party on June 5, 2013 (not published as a document)

Date of approval of the Opinion: March 30, 2016

Subject matter: Criminal conviction and confiscation of assets of the authors

On the merits: Right of liberty; guarantees of due process; retroactive application of unfavorable criminal law; equality before the law and non-discrimination

---

[*] Adopted by the Committee in its 116th session (March 7-31, 2016).

[**] Adopted by the Committee in its 116th session (March 7-31, 2016).

On procedure: Lack of status as victim; inadmissibility *ratione materiae*; *litis pendentia*; lack of jurisdiction; non-exhaustion of domestic remedies; abuse of the right to submit communications

Articles of the Covenant: 2(1) y (3a); 9; 14(1) (2) and (3c); 15; 26

Articles of the Optional Protocol: 1; 3; 5(2) a) and b)

1. The authors of the communication are Roberto Isaías Dassum and William Isaías Dassum, Ecuadorian citizens. They allege that they are victims of the violation of their rights recognized in Articles 9; 14(1) and (2), separately and in relation to Article 2(1) and (3a); 14(3c); 15; and 26 of the International Covenant on Civil and Political Rights. The Optional Protocol went into force for Ecuador on March 23, 1976.

The facts according to the authors

2.1 The authors are businessmen and were shareholders and administrators of companies comprising a corporate unit known as the "Isaías Group," the most visible head of which was Filanbanco bank. The authors were President and Vice President of this bank, respectively. At the end of the nineties, Ecuador went through external and internal difficulties that seriously affected its economy. The loss of the manufacturing sector in general had severe repercussions on the financial system, as creditor of the former. Ecuadorian banks suffered a serious crisis starting in 1998, when practically all of the banks requested liquidity loans from the Central Bank of Ecuador (Banco Central del Ecuador – BCE). These loans were granted by the BCE in 1998 and were based on the solvency of the regulatory capital constituted by the financial group in question, which was sent to the Office of the Superintendent of Banks. The solvency of Filanbanco was certified by that entity, which approved its access to stabilization loans.

2.2 After receiving several liquidity loans, the private shareholders of Filanbanco asked the Ecuadorean Banking Board to have the bank undergo a Restructuring Program in order to strengthen it, which was decided by a Resolution dated December 2, 1998. This program applied exclusively to solvent banks facing liquidity problems, which proves that Filanbanco was a solvent bank whose liquidity problems were temporary. Otherwise it would have undergone a sanitization process [*procedimiento de saneamiento*] for subsequent liquidation.

2.3 Under the Restructuring Program, the bank was turned over to a state agency, the Deposit Guarantee Agency (Agencia de Garantía de Depósitos – AGD). An audit performed by entity *Arthur Andersen* in March 1999, just three months after the bank was turned over to the AGD and during the state administration, demonstrated that the bank was solvent and that the private administration crisis was due to liquidity problems. However, on July 30, 2002, while still under state administration, the Banking Board ordered the forced liquidation of the bank, not without first requiring Filanbanco to absorb an insolvent bank (Banco La Previsora), and making Filanbanco give loans to other banks in difficulty. Faced with the declaration of forced liquidation, Filanbanco closed its doors to the public on July 30, 2002. On April 8, 2010, the Office of the Superintendent of Banks declared that its assets would be transferred to the BCE and its legal personality extinguished.

2.4 Within the framework of the facts described, intense persecution came about against the authors as former shareholders and administrators of Filanbanco, including threats and defamation by the Office of the President of the country and other government officials, and the start of a criminal proceeding. The proceeding was started with the request sent by the Prosecutor General to the Chief Justice of the Supreme Court on June 16, 2000, for him to institute proceedings against the authors and other former Filanbanco officials for the offenses of bank peculation [*peculado*] (Article 257 of the Criminal Code in effect at the time of the perpetration of the facts, i.e. 1998˚), and forgery (Article 363 of the same Code), as well as several financial offenses provided for in the General Law on Financial Institutions. On June 22, 2000, the Chief Justice of the Court issued an order to begin instituting proceedings for the offenses mentioned by the prosecutor and ordered the authors remanded in custody. On June 26, 2000, the Chief Justice of the Court sent an arrest warrant to the General Command of the National Police, which order was appealed by the authors on June 27, 2000.

2.5 On November 20, 2002, upon completing the investigation of the facts, the Prosecutor General filed her Formal Charge, which amends her report of June 16, 2000 in light of the investigation. The Charge contains the accusation against the authors for financial offenses (false statements and authorization of unlawful operations), but states that there was no abuse of public funds belonging to the BCE (peculation) or bank peculation, since the

---

* Article 257: "(…) the punishment for servants of public sector organizations and entities and any person in charge of a public service, who has abused public or private monies, paper representing them, instruments, certificates, documents or securities that were in their possession by virtue of or due to their position shall be imprisonment of four to eight years; whether the abuse consists of misappropriation [desfalco], arbitrary disposal or any other similar form (…).
This provision shall include servants who handle funds of the Ecuadorian Social Security Institute or of government or private banks (…)."
Law No. 99-26 of May 13, 1999 introduced an amendment which added the following section:
"Also included in the provisions of this article are officials, administrators, executives and employees of the private national financial system, as well as directors or members of the supervisory boards and boards of directors of these entities, who have contributed to the perpetration of these offenses."
The same law added the criminal classification of "special bank peculation":
Art. 257 A: "The punishment for persons described in the previous article who, in abusing their status, acted fraudulently to obtain or grant related loans shall be imprisonment of four to eight years, whether such loans are related or intercompany, thereby violating express legal provisions regarding this type of transaction (…)".

granting of connected loans [*créditos vinculados*], be they related or intercompany, was classified as peculation (banking) only after the alleged facts.

2.6 On March 19, 2003, the Chief Justice of the Court, departing from the accusation brought by the Prosecutor General, issued an order to stand trial for the offense of bank peculation*. Against this order, the authors filed remedies of appeal and procedural nullity before the Chief Justice of the Court.

2.7 On May 12, 2009, the First Criminal Division of the National Court of Justice (National Court) upheld the order to stand trial. The authors requested supplemental information, clarifications, amendments, declarations of nullity, and the recusal of the judges. On October 28, 2009, the judges comprising the division decided to recuse themselves from continuing to hear the case, arguing that they had received bribery attempts. To replace them, three associate justices were named, who ruled on the authors' appeals in a ruling dated January 15, 2010. Furthermore, they amended the order to stand trial dated May 12, 2009, arguing that the principles of lawfulness and congruence between the formal accusation and the judgment had been violated. Consequently, the authors should not be tried for peculation but for the offenses they were charged with in the formal accusation (balance sheets and forgery of documents).

2.8 On January 19, 2010, the Chief Justice of the National Court of Justice suspended the three associate judges at his initiative due to "alleged irregularities that have generated social unrest, affecting the image of the Judicial Function," and began disciplinary proceedings against them for changing the criminal classification with which the authors were charged. The President of

---

* The ruling indicates that in certain media it was maintained that bank peculation existed only as of the introduction of Article 257A of the criminal code. However, this assertion is baseless, since the classification of bank peculation was already described in section 3 of Article 257, which was in force at the time the facts were committed. The ruling cites a judgment issued in 1984 in which the Supreme Court applied said criminal provision and convicted the administrators of Banco La Previsora.

the Republic asked the National Court of Justice to investigate the associate judges' accounts and publicly declared that the National Court of Justice should dismiss them. On January 26, 2010, the National Assembly issued a resolution rejecting the ruling by the associate judges, and it exhorted the National Court of Justice to investigate their actions and decide on the corresponding sanctions. The associate judges wound up being indicted by the Prosecutor General in the National Court of Justice, removed and tried for the offense of perversion of justice [*prevaricato*]. The trial against them was nevertheless dismissed by the Second Criminal Division of the National Court on December 8, 2010, due to lack of evidence.

2.9 The vacancy created by the removal of the associate judges was filled with the appointment of a "Criminal Division of Provisional Associate Judges of the National Court of Justice," created specifically for this proceeding. The Constitution establishes a single category of associate judges in the National Court, who are selected with the same proceedings and the same responsibilities as regular judges; they are appointed by the National Court of Justice through a public competition (not hand-picked by the Chief Justice of the National Court); and their function is not that of judging a specific case*.

---

* According to the May 17, 2010 decision issued by the temporary associate judges, contained in the case file before the Committee, the Prosecutor General appealed the ruling by the panel of permanent associate judges, requesting their removal and the upholding of the order issued by the regular judges. The appeal was ruled on by the panel of temporary associate judges by virtue of the rules governing the functioning of the National Court, in particular the Court's ruling of January 21, 2009, which gives the Presiding Justice of the Court the option to appoint temporary associate judges when neither the regular judges nor the permanent associate judges can act. With their jurisdiction established, the temporary associate judges ascertained that the panel of permanent associate judges had amended at their own initiative the decision by the permanent judges to process the authors for peculation without having the authority to do so, since regardless of the composition of the court, it was the same jurisdictional body and, therefore, it could not overturn its own decision. Its competence was limited to

2.10 On May 17, 2010, this Division declared the decision of January 15, 2010 non-existent and reinstated the charge of peculation. This was the only decision by the Division. After issuing it, its members returned to their private occupations as attorneys.

2.11 The facts involved in the proceeding occurred before 1998, when the Constitution of 1979 and the Code of Criminal Procedure of 1983 were in effect. According to Articles 254 and 255 of this Code, the proceeding is to be stayed until the defendants surrender or are captured for their trial. On August 11, 1998, a new Constitution went into effect, Article 12 of which set forth the trial in absentia of officials and civil servants in general accused of offenses of peculation, bribery, extortion, and unlawful enrichment. The 2008 Constitution contains a similar provision. The authors were not public officials nor were they being investigated for the offenses mentioned. In addition, the facts with which they were charged had occurred before the Constitution of 1998, in spite of which the proceeding against them continued.

2.12 On August 3, 2010, the Second Criminal Division of the National Court ordered that the trial begin. In addition, it ratified the remand order for the authors and the order instructing police authorities and the Interpol to locate and apprehend them. On August 11, 2010, the authors' appeals were denied, and the proceeding in absentia was ordered to begin. In parallel, the Government requested and obtained from Interpol multiple international arrest warrants against the authors, who were living in the United States. In addition, the Government asked the United States to extradite them.

2.13 On April 10, 2012, a judge of the Specialized Criminal Division of the National Court sentenced the authors to eight years of imprisonment for the offense of peculation. The remedies of

---

ruling on occasional petitions for clarification or supplemental information brought by defendants. Consequently, the panel of temporary associate judges declared the order by the permanent associate judges as non-existent and declared the order by the regular judges in force. With regard to the defendant's petitions for clarification and supplemental information, the panel rejected them for not being related to defects of language or clarification.

appeal, nullity and cassation were denied on March 12, April 24 and October 29, 2014, respectively, by the Specialized Criminal Division. The Constitutional Court declared on September 17, 2015 contested the processing of an extraordinary action for protection.

2.14 The National Court at its own initiative quashed the judgment on appeal that found the authors liable for the offense of peculation – due to misuse [*malversación*] – as classified in Article 257 of the Criminal Code, deeming that said judgment erroneously interpreted that article and that the offense for which the authors were convicted was in reality bank peculation, as provided for in the same article. The penalty imposed was eight years in prison, with no attenuating circumstances, in light of the existence of the aggravating factor of acting as a gang [*pandilla*] to commit the offense.

2.15 According to the authors, the judgment on cassation worsens the violations of the Covenant since: (a) It violates the principle of lawfulness, by retroactively applying "misuse" as the form of the offense of peculation, a crime that had been decriminalized; it retroactively applied the least favorable criminal law, since it considered them active parties in the criminal classification of bank peculation, which at the time of the accusation applied to much more limited crimes; it applied the aggravating 'gang' factor, which was revoked in the current Organic Comprehensive Criminal Code; and applied the criminal classification of peculation, which is indeterminate and hinders the accused from defending themselves; (b) It violates the right of formal equality, by applying more burdensome penalties than those that would have been imposed in identical cases; (c) It violates the principle of *non reformatio in peius*, by imposing more burdensome penalties and different offenses than those contained in the judgment on appeal, thereby violating the right of defense; (d) it violates the right to be judged by independent judges, since the judges who decided the appeal on points of law had already participated in previous decisions on the same case or had publicly demonstrated partiality toward it.

2.16 In parallel with the criminal proceeding, a civil proceeding took place to confiscate assets, carried out by the AGD against the former shareholders and former administrators of Filanbanco, for the alleged purpose of guaranteeing payment of the credit of bank depositors at the time of its intervention. The proceeding was begun by means of Resolution AGD-UIO-GG-2008-12 dated July 8, 2008, which ordered the confiscation of all the assets owned by those who were administrators and shareholders of Filanbanco up to December 2, 1998. On this basis, with no prior administrative or judicial proceeding and with the support of law enforcement, the confiscation of more than 200 companies and other assets owned by the authors and other members of the Isaías group began[*]. In addition, on July 9, 2008, the Constituent Assembly, elected within the framework of the political proceeding led by the President of the Republic, issued Constituent Mandate No. 13, which it endowed with constitutional stature. This mandate ratified the legal validity of the abovementioned Resolution; it declared that the Resolution would not be subject to an action for constitutional protection or any other special action; and it ordered that the filed actions be closed, without compliance with being able to stay or prevent the Resolution. Judges hearing any class of constitutional action regarding this ruling and those made to enforce it should declare them inadmissible, or face removal, notwithstanding any criminal liability that may be pertinent. The Mandate also stipulated that it was not "open to complaint, appeal, action for protection, petition, claim, or any administrative or judicial judgment or ruling whatsoever".

2.17 The precedent for Mandate No. 13 is Constitutional Mandate No. 1, dated November 9, 2007, which prohibits oversight or appeal of the decisions of the Constituent Assembly. This Mandate stipulates that judges and courts that process any action contrary to those decisions will be removed and face trial. On June 10, 2010, Roberto Isaías Dassum filed a petition of unconstitutionality before the Constitutional Court against Mandate No. 13 which was dismissed on June 21, 2012, based on the immunity enjoyed by the Mandate.

---

* The case file contains a list of companies and other assets confiscated.

2.18 The remedies filed by the authors against this Resolution and others that followed aimed at confiscating assets were unsuccessful. The Resolution states that all assets of the authors were subject to confiscation, including those that were not earmarked for the operation of Filanbanco or any other company in that economic group, i.e. also those allocated for the authors' personal use. In addition, the confiscation encompassed assets that were deemed property of the authors according to public knowledge, i.e. regardless of the title indicated in the respective property deeds.

The complaint

3.1 The authors argue that the irregularities occurring in the criminal proceeding and in the proceeding to confiscate their assets resulted in violations of their right to the judicial guarantees of due process under Article 14, paragraphs 1, 2 and 3 c), separately and in relation to Articles 2, paragraphs 1 and 3 a); and the right of equality before the law and of non-discrimination under Article 26; the right not to suffer a retroactively applied unfavorable criminal law, under Article 15; and the right to personal liberty pursuant to Article 9 of the Covenant.

3.2 The case is not pending before another international court and the domestic remedies in the criminal proceeding have been exhausted. With respect to the confiscation proceeding, no appropriate judicial remedy exists, since Constituent Mandate No. 13 excluded any judicial action or remedy.

Complaints regarding Articles 14 and 26

3.3 In the criminal proceeding, Ecuador violated the authors' rights to: (i) be judged by a competent, independent and impartial court, established by law; (ii) being presumed innocent until proven guilty; and (iii) being judged without undue delays.

3.4 The decision by the three permanent associate judges of the First Criminal Division of the National Court not to process the authors for the offense of bank peculation prompted their removal and prosecution. Such arbitrariness infringes the judicial independence stipulated in Article 14(1) of the Covenant.

3.5 The panel of provisional associate judges created specifically for this proceeding reestablished the charge of "bank peculation." This decision was made only ten days after the associate judges were sworn in, despite the complexity of the case, the size of the case file and after 10 years of duration of the case. It was the only ruling issued by this panel. It was an ad hoc court, therefore, created in violation of the requirements provided for by law for the sole purpose of issuing a ruling against the authors. Whatever the basis of domestic law that is invoked for the constitution of this "temporary" court, it is unlawful for it to have been exclusively to take the place of the three associate judges who were arbitrarily suspended and removed. Consequently, the appointment of this panel violated the principle of a "competent court established by law."

3.6 On May 10, 2010, Roberto Isaías requested the revocation of the appointment of the temporary associate judges. On May 11 and 20, 2010, respectively, he requested that these associate judges recuse themselves from hearing the case and appealed the decision that reinstated the accusation of bank peculation, arguing violation of the right to be judged by a competent, independent and impartial court

3.7 The guarantee of the natural judge was also violated, since, because they were domiciled in Guayaquil, the authors should have been tried by an ordinary court in the District of Guayas. However, the case against the authors was joined to those of other persons who had venue, so as to take the proceeding to the National Court.

3.8 Violation of the right to an impartial judge or court occurred also due to the prohibition for the authors to recuse judges. This prohibition was the result of an amendment to the Code of Criminal Procedure introduced in 2009 establishing an absolute impediment to the recusal of judges on cases begun and processed under the Code of 1983, which was the one applicable to the case against the authors.

3.9 The authors' right under Article 14(2) of the Covenant to the presumption of innocence was violated as a result of: (i) repeated statements by the highest officials of the Executive Branch asserting their guilt; and (ii) the treatment that the authors received as guilty parties during the proceeding, even before being judged in the trial phase. Already in the order opening the trial the Chief Justice of the Supreme Court asserted that "it had been determined in the trial" that the authors "had committed" acts that "constituted offenses that are means for the perpetration of the offence of bank peculation." These and other assertions of the same tenor implied considering the authors' guilt as proven before starting the oral trial and put them in the position of having the burden to show during the rest of the proceedings that they were not guilty.

3.10 The right of the authors to be judged without undue delays was infringed by the unreasonable duration of the proceeding: (i) four years after the occurrence of the charged facts and two years after the start of the proceeding, in order for the formal accusation to be issued (November 20, 2002); and (ii) more than six years to rule on the appeal against the order opening the trial, even though the law stipulates that it must be ruled on within 15 days plus one additional day for every 100 pages of the case file. Between the formal start of the trial and its ratification by the panel of temporary associate judges more than seven years passed.

3.11 The authors' absence from the country cannot be invoked as grounds for delay in the criminal proceeding, for two reasons: a) the State chose to judge them in absentia, even though its own Constitution prohibited it; and b) upon leaving Ecuador, the authors exercised their lawful right to safeguard their liberty, integrity and safety in view of the abuse of power to which they were subject.

3.12 In the confiscations proceeding, the right to due process also was violated. The AGD is an administrative body that does not elude the scope of Article 14 of the Covenant when it engages in activities designed to determine civil rights and obligations. Bearing this in mind, the lack of an adversarial administrative proceeding before the AGD, where the authors could exercise their right to defense before the AGD decided to confiscate their assets violated the guarantees of due process (Article 14(1) and (2) of the Covenant). The State shielded the legal weakness of Resolution AGD-UIOGG-2008-12 through Mandate No. 13, endowing it with jurisdictional immunity. This immunity presupposes a violation of the right of access to justice, to due process and to equality before the law and the courts to claim civil rights, specifically the property rights of the authors as former owners and shareholders of Filanbanco. Mandate No. 13 also violates the right to due process in relation to Article 2, paragraphs 1 and 3 a) of the Covenant, in not respecting the right to file an effective appeal and the right of the authors to equality before the court. For the same reasons the Resolution and Mandate No. 13 jointly violate the right of equality before the law and non-discrimination as provided for in Article 26 of the Covenant, in denying access to justice for specific persons for them to claim their rights*

Complaints concerning Article 15

3.13 The authors are victims of the violation of this article due to: (i) their being subject to the application *ex post facto* of a new criminal classification and (ii) a criminal classification was applied to them which had already been revoked at the time of the start of the trial phase of the criminal proceeding.

3.14 By means of Law No.99-26 of May 13, 1999, i.e. after the charged facts took place, the Criminal Code was amended to include the criminal classification of "special bank peculation" (Article 257-A), which did not exist until then and which implies the execution of loan transactions with related companies. This amendment shows that, prior to it, the conduct described by this offense was not punishable. Until that date, both the banking legislation and the criminal law expressly allowed those transactions within certain limits. Now, the National Court applied the revoked criminal classification (Article 257) to the authors, yet

---

* The authors state that a claim against the Resolution filed on June 28, 2010 was rejected by the Provincial Court of Justice of Guayaquil in application of Mandate No. 13.

changed its interpretation and classified under it related-party and intercompany transactions. The prohibition of retroactive application of Article 15(1) of the Covenant cannot be avoided through an extensive or wrongful interpretation of an old law for the purpose of endowing the new law with retroactive effect.

3.15 Furthermore, the authors were charged with having authorized the use of the liquidity loans granted by the BCE to Filanbanco for purposes other than those provided for by law. This conduct dovetails with the legal definition of misuse. Now, Law 2001-47, "decriminalized" misuse of public or private funds as a form of peculation, before the order to stand trial was issued against the authors in 2003. So there is a violation of Article 15(1) *in fine* of the Covenant, which protects the right to retroactive application of the most favorable criminal law. This is despite the fact that the Supreme Court avoided employing the term "misuse," instead using the terms "arbitrary disposal of public funds" and "fraud" through the "authorization of unlawful financial transactions".

3.16 In the confiscations proceeding started on July 8, 2008, there was also retroactivity contrary to Article 15(1), since the legal basis used by the AGD was Article 29 of the Law of Reorganization on Economic Matters in the Financial Tax Area, introduced therein in 2002.

Complaints concerning Article 9

3.17 The judicial decision of remanding the authors into custody, although not consummated, is an arbitrary measure by the State contrary to Article 9 of the Covenant. In order for individual liberty to be violated, it is not always necessary for an order of remand into custody to be executed materially, nor does the person subject to an arbitrary detention order against him have to suffer incarceration. The mere issuance of the imprisonment order of June 22, 2000 and of an international arrest warrant, as well as the other proceedings to obtain capture, such as extradition proceedings, within the framework of an irregular, arbitrary criminal proceeding devoid of the least judicial guarantees, violates the right to personal liberty.

The State party's observations on admissibility

4.1 In its observations of December 4, 2013 and December 10, 2015, the State party sets forth the differences between the criminal proceeding (started in 2000) and the confiscations proceeding (started in 2008). Within the former, the necessary judicial guarantees were provided, since the criminal case is directed against natural persons for presumably criminal activities governed by the Criminal Code. On the other hand, the facts associated with the confiscation of assets originate with business activities and actions related to the assets of legal persons. Given that in the proceeding before the Committee, the only complainants are the authors, no domestic action other than these may be introduced in said proceeding. Only natural persons have the right to the international protection of human rights. Consequently, proceedings having legal persons as plaintiffs, wherein their rights and obligations in relation to national laws are discussed, must remain outside of the subject of the communication. In addition, it is not fitting to discuss actions that have been filed by persons other than the authors, whether legal or natural.

4.2 Although the communication alleges the violation of rights under the Covenant, it does so from the presumed confiscation of assets of companies or groups of companies, which pertains to legal persons. The authors attempt to extend the rights of the Covenant to defend legal persons' rights. For this reason, the Committee must declare its lack of jurisdiction over any administrative, legal or jurisdictional fact involving companies or business groups. In addition, the allegations associated with the rights of ownership of shareholders, administrators, companies and corporate units such as the Isaías Group are for the purpose of protecting an alleged property right, meaning the allegations related to the confiscations proceedings must be found inadmissible by the Committee due to the subject matter.

4.3 The authors filed an application with the Inter-American

Commission on Human Rights. Its processing took place with the ruling not to open the case due to not meeting the requirements for its consideration nor the exhaustion of domestic remedies. The Commission performed a prolix analysis of the petition and adopted a final decision duly notified to the complainants. Consequently, it is up to the Committee not to hear the communication, in accordance with Article 5, paragraph 2 a) of the Optional Protocol.

4.4 The communication lacks support insofar as the State's obligations in accordance with the Covenant, given that the authors are not within Ecuadorian territory and therefore the obligations of the Covenant cannot be enforced on the State party. For the same reason, the authors are not subject to the State's law enforcement.

4.5 The Optional Protocol stipulates as an exception to the exhaustion of remedies unjustified delay in the processing of a remedy. In this case, the complexity of the proceeding must be taken into account, in which it was necessary to request and subsequently analyze extensive technical reports (outside audits) and reports by different public supervisory institutions (Central Bank, Anti-Corruption Commission, Office of the Superintendent of Banks, and the Office of the Supervisor of Banks). In addition, the proceeding was carried out within a reasonable time period if we take into account the intense procedural activity by the authors, who filed every type of remedy within the criminal proceeding in accordance with domestic law[*].

4.6 The authors have come before the Committee without taking into account the objective of the Covenant and the Optional Protocol, obstructing the work of hearing individual petitions submitted before this body. It is a clear example of an abuse of the right that they have to submit a communication.

State party's observations on the merits

---

[*] The State party provides a chronological list of the procedural motions occurring during the years in which the proceeding was pending.

4.7 Any argument by the authors questioning the independence of the judges and courts is merely the result of their dissatisfaction with court decisions and does not derive from the obligations set forth in Article 14 of the Covenant. Article 182 of the Ecuadorian Constitution stipulates the figure of associate judges as part of the judicial structure, with the same rank and the same regime of conflicts of interest and responsibilities in the performance of their function as regular judges. Based on the regulatory power of the Full National Court, contained in the Ruling by the Constitutional Court for the transitional period, with status as binding constitutional case law for all civil servants and private individuals, the Substitute Ruling on the Composition of the National Court date December 22, 2008 was issued, Article 11 of which determines the legitimate, legal and constitutional activity of the associate judges of the National Court. This provision states that "in the absence of permanent associate judges, temporary judges can be called upon to hear a given case. The appointment will fall to the judges comprising the Division where it is tried and absent them, to the Presiding Judge of the respective Division." Consequently, the right of any person to be heard by a competent court has not been violated. Furthermore, the recusal of judges as a tool of procedural guarantee is in effect in Ecuador.

4.8 There was no violation of the principle of presumption of innocence due to the statements of the President of the Republic, made in a space intended for informing citizens about his activities and the policies of the Government, which space represents the freedom of expression of all citizens, including the chief executive, whose personal opinions about a given subject do not imply influence over judges and courts.

4.9 With respect to the complaints regarding Article 15, the offense of peculation was already classified in the criminal code of 1938, subsequently amended in 1971 (Article 257). This provision was amended once again in 1977. In keeping therewith, "servants of state or private banks" began to be considered as active parties, and even included shareholders, administrators, and employees*. This made it possible to prosecute the authors and other bankers of the time. The judge deemed the authors to be private banking servants who were active as President and Vice President of Filanbanco, and who according to the judgment on appeal "abused public funds, i.e. the liquidity loans granted by the Central Bank (...) subsuming their conduct under the offense of peculation classified and sanctioned in the first and second sections of Article 257". Subsequently, the law of May 13, 1999, added a third section to this article, including therein "officials, administrators, executives or employees of institutions of the private financial system, as well as directors or members of the supervisory boards and boards of directors of these entities". The amendment clarified what was previously stipulated in relation to active parties under the criminal classification. The lawmaker, in view of the social unrest created by the serious economic, social and political consequences of the banking crisis of 1998, sought through this amendment to expressly determine the active parties of the offense, without this implying that the previous provision had not contemplated them.

4.10 With respect to the confiscations proceeding, the AGD and the Banking Board observed the principle of legality. Specifically, AGD Resolution 153 of July 31, 2008 contains the Instructions for the Confiscation of Assets and guarantees processing with observation of the rules of due process, wherefore there is no violation whatsoever of Article 14(1) of the Covenant in relation to the equality of persons before the courts. Moreover, the confiscations system had procedures for proving the lawful origin and the real ownership of the assets confiscated. The AGD in the alleged abusive exercise of power could have been subjected to a review of administrative remedies contained in the Law on Administrative Courts.

4.11 With respect to Constituent Mandate No. 13, Ecuador rejects the authors' argument regarding its unconstitutionality and unlawfulness. The Constituent Assembly was not a state body but rather a supra-state, whose mandate derives directly from

---

* Finding of the National Court in the judgment on cassation.

the people's will. According to the democratic principle, this will is of a different nature and clearly superior to the State. According to Article 2.2 of its Regulations, "the Constituent National Assembly will approve Constituent Mandates that restrict its decisions and provisions in the exercise of full powers. The Mandates will have immediate effect notwithstanding their publication in the respective medium". The Assembly considered the complex financial and administrative situation of Filanbanco and emphasized the importance of the management of State institutions (AGD), considered part of the expression of the powers constituted in the eradication of any form of impunity. These circumstances legitimized the asset confiscation proceeding. Within Mandate No. 13, the Assembly issued measures for the protection of the rights of workers at companies under receivership [*empresas intervenidas*], through a Resolution dated July 8, 2008. The Resolution and Mandate No. 13 are acts by the State that contain *ad-hominen* legal provisions, since they do not refer to natural persons, as the authors maintain.

4.12 Since the authors are neither under Ecuador's jurisdiction nor within its territory, facts related to alleged violation of Article 9 of the Covenant cannot be attributed to Ecuador. With respect to the extradition proceeding, in June 2013 the United States State Department informed the Ecuadorian State of its refusal to extradite the authors, indicating that Ecuador had to provide sufficient evidence to find probable cause for the offense charged, and that the Departments of State and Justice would give subsequent consideration to the extradition request.

4.13 The State party recalls the Committee's jurisdiction in the case González del Río v. Perú (communication 263/1987), according to which the issuance or existence of a remand order does not in and of itself constitute custody. This case law reaffirms that the scope of protection of the right in question is physical liberty and that its violation not only requires that detention of the affected person be carried out but also that such detention be illegal and/or arbitrary. To the extent that the competent judge issues a remand order in accordance with legal provisions and justifies the existence of evidence of existence of the offense and participation by the defendants in its perpetration, as it appeared in the warrant to initiate proceedings issued in the criminal proceeding against the authors, the precautionary measure of remand into custody is justified. The order dated June 22, 2000 justified the order for remand into custody due to non-compliance with the law by Filanbanco, for during the effective period of the loans granted by the Central Bank, these were not used to safeguard the stability of the financial system, but to invest in prohibited transactions. Throughout the criminal proceeding, the order for remand into custody was analyzed periodically by the judges on the case for the purpose of verifying its nature and ensuring that the defendants appeared in court. Each ratification of the order met the legal requirements and was justified by the evidence of the existence of offenses. Furthermore, the effective period of the orders for remand into custody weighing on a person who is a fugitive cannot be computed, for the order itself does not constitute a limitation of their physical liberty, nor can it prove or become unlawful or arbitrary.

Authors' comments on the State party's observations

5.1 The authors made comments on the State party's observations dated February 6, 2014.

5.2 The smear campaign and the continual statements against them have continued. Thus, in February 2014, through the Enlace Ciudadano program, broadcasts by different radio and television media, the President of the Republic once again accused them of bankrupting the country's most important bank and attacking the national government in the media, referring to them as "villains" and "criminals".

5.3 Ecuador asserts that in the criminal proceeding all the guarantees of due process and judicial protection were met. However, it offers no support for such statement, does not discredit the facts set forth in the communication, and does not undermine their being characterized as the violation of rights guaranteed by the Covenant.

5.4 With regard to the observations on the confiscation proceeding, the authors note that behind the right of legal persons are the rights of the natural persons, their shareholders, who the State itself decided as the authors or their family members. The Law on Reorganization on Economic Matters in the Financial Tax Area expressly provides a measure against "shareholders," who would be liable with their personal assets, i.e. as individuals or natural persons, for alleged bank debts, i.e. the legal persons where they serve as partners as individuals. All of the State's actions reported in this communication were expressly directed against the authors as individuals and not against a legal person.

5.5 With respect to the proceeding before the Inter-American Commission on Human Rights, the authors submitted their complaint in 2005, but in 2008 the Commission decided not to open it for processing due to the lack of exhaustion of domestic remedies. The authors requested reconsideration, but subsequently abandoned and formally withdrew their application. This occurred before they submitted their communication to the Committee.

5.6 The authors reject Ecuador's argument regarding lack of jurisdiction for reasons of territory. All of the acts reported in the communication were executed by agents of the State in exercising Ecuadorian jurisdiction. Their absence from the territory does not exempt the State from liability for violating its obligations under the Covenant, nor does it remove the victims from the protection they enjoy under the Covenant. Trying a person entails exercising the State's jurisdiction and power over them.

5.7 Ecuador does not provide evidence of the existence of the abuse of law, nor does it explain how it allegedly occurred. With respect to the delay in the criminal proceeding, it is ascribable to the lack of diligence of the judicial authorities and the arbitrariness of their actions, which has forced the authors to file remedies to defend their procedural guarantees.

5.8 As one of the causes of the financial crisis of 1999-2000, Ecuador mentions the deregulation and freeing up of financial activity which reduced the State's control over that sector. This assertion shows that the activities and behaviors for which the authors were tried were not prohibited by the legislation then in effect. To the contrary, they were consistent with the General Law on Institutions of the Financial System.

5.9 With respect to the proceeding's duration, the authors state that not filing remedies and not exercising defenses cannot be a negative burden suffered by the victims of procedural violations. The delay of six years after the issuance of the order to stand trial for the start of the criminal trial cannot be attributed to the authors, nor can it be justified that a proceeding to determine liability for banking offenses should have taken more than 13 years.

5.10 The Organic Code of the Judicial Function, dated March 9, 2009, does not grant the National Court jurisdiction to appoint temporary associate judges and it revokes the Supreme Court Ruling of May 19, 2008 that allowed for the appointment of temporary associate judges.

5.11 With respect to Mandate No. 13, the authors recall that the objective of a Constituent Assembly is to draft a new constitution. In certain cases, these bodies have taken on some other functions, for example, the appointment of officials or the promulgation of certain transitory provisions between one constitutional order and the next. However, the fact that a constituent body should govern and affect specific cases, of specific persons, depriving them of fundamental rights, constitutes an irregular and discriminatory situation.

5.12 With respect to the non-application of an ex post facto or revoked criminal classification, Ecuador did not provide a precise answer to the authors' allegations, nor did it discredit their arguments with respect to the violation of Article 15(1) *in fine* of the Covenant. With regard to the complaint under Article 9 of the Covenant, the authors reiterate their initial arguments. The remand order against them remains in effect, and Ecuador continues trying to physically deprive them of liberty.

The Committee's deliberations

Admissibility examination

6.1 Before examining any complaint put forth in a communication, the Human Rights Committee must decide, in accordance with Article 93 of its regulations, whether or not the case is admissible by virtue of the Optional Protocol to the Covenant.

6.2 The Committee hereby notes the objection put forth by the State party that the Covenant's obligations are not enforceable on it since the authors are not within Ecuadorian territory, the Committee believes that the authors' complaints are related to court proceedings brought against them in the State party, regardless of their residence abroad, and that on this matter the State party has exercised its jurisdiction. Consequently, absence from the territory does not constitute an obstacle to the admissibility of the communication.

6.3 The Committee finds that the authors' allegations are not of a nature to imply abuse of the right to submit communications and that no obstacles exist to the admissibility of the communication under Article 3 of the Optional Protocol.

6.4 The Committee hereby notes the State party's observations that the communication is inadmissible by virtue of Article 5, paragraph 2 a), of the Optional Protocol, because the authors filed a complaint before the Inter-American Commission on Human Rights. The authors responded to this argument noting that the Commission decided in 2008 not to open the complaint to processing; and that the authors requested its reconsideration but then withdrew their application, before submitting their communication to the Committee. The Committee recalls its case law* and finds that said matter is not being examined within the framework of another international examination or settlement proceeding. Therefore, the

Committee is not prevented under Article 5, paragraph 2 a) of the Optional Protocol from examining this communication.

6.5 The authors state that the court decision to remand them in custody violates their rights under Article 9 of the Covenant. The Committee observes, however, that the remand order was issued

---

* Communication 2202/2012, *Castañeda v. México*, decision of admissibility of July 18, 2013, paragraph 6.3.

within the framework of a criminal proceeding, that it has not been executed since the authors are not within the territory of the State party, and that the authors are not remanded into custody. Consequently, the Committee finds that this complaint is without basis and is inadmissible in accordance with Article 2 of the Optional Protocol.

6.6 With respect to the complaints relative to Articles 14(1) and (2) of the Covenant, separately, and in relation to Articles 2(1) and (3a); and 26 with regard to the asset confiscation proceeding; and Articles 14(1)(2) and (3c) and 15 of the Covenant in relation to the criminal proceeding, the Committee deems that they have been sufficiently well-founded for purposes of admissibility, declares them admissible and proceeds to examine them on the merits.

Examination of the matter on the merits

7.1 The Human Rights Committee has examined this communication taking into account all the information the parties have provided to it, in accordance with the requirements of Article 5, paragraph 1, of the Optional Protocol.

7.2 The authors argue that the asset confiscation proceeding violated their right of access to justice, to equality before the courts and to due process under Article 14(1) and (2) of the Covenant in the determination of their civil rights to appeal the confiscation of assets of their personal property; that there was no adversarial administrative proceeding in which they could exercise their right to defense before the AGD decided to undertake the confiscation; that Constituent Mandate No. 13 prohibited the filing of legal actions against the AGD resolution that ordered the confiscations and expressly established that judges hearing any class of constitutional action concerning that resolution and those adopted to enforce it should dismiss them, subject to removal, notwithstanding the criminal liability that may be pertinent; and that these issues also violated their right of due process in relation to Article 2(1) and (3a), and the right to equality before the law and to non-discrimination in accordance with Article 26. The State party notes that the facts associated with the confiscation of assets originated with business activities and actions related to the assets of legal persons. Given that only natural persons have the right to international protection in terms of human rights, the authors' complaints regarding the confiscations proceeding would fall outside of the subject matter of the communication; also on account of the subject matter, since the objective of complaints is an alleged right to property.

7.3 The Committee recalls its General Comment No. 31 (2004) on the Nature of the General Legal Obligation on States Parties to the Covenant, in paragraph 9 of which it is stated that "the fact that the competence of the Committee to receive and consider communications is restricted to those submitted by or on behalf of individuals (Article 1 of the Optional Protocol) does not prevent such individuals from claiming that actions or omissions that concern legal persons and similar entities amount to a violation of their own rights".

7.4 In this case, the Committee deems that the issuance of Constituent Mandate No. 13, which expressly prohibited the filing of an action for constitutional protection or another special action against the resolutions of the AGD and included the instruction to remove, without prejudice of the criminal liability that could be pertinent, the judges who heard this type of actions, violated the authors' rights under Article 14 (1) of the Covenant, to a proceeding with the due guarantees in the determination of their civil rights or obligations.

7.5 Having reached this conclusion, the Committee will not examine the complaint concerning violation of Article 26 of the Covenant due to the same facts.

7.6 The authors assert that the criminal proceeding violated their rights under Article 14 to be tried by a competent, independent and impartial court, established by law; to the presumption of innocence; and to be tried without undue delays. In this regard, the Committee notes that the National Court was designated as competent in light of the venue some of the co-defendants had and on the basis of domestic procedural provisions, interpretations of which the Committee is not responsible for calling into question.

7.7 The Committee also notes that the formal charge of November 20, 2002 accused the authors of financial offenses but not of peculation, noting, among other things, that bank peculation had been classified subsequent to the charged facts. However, the Chief Justice of the Court issued the order to stand trial for the offense of bank peculation, asserting that said conduct was indeed included in Article 257 of the Criminal Code in effect at the time of the facts and that case law existed in that regard. The order to stand trial for this offense was upheld on May 12, 2009 by the Criminal Division of the Court; however, the judges comprising this Division subsequently recused themselves from continuing to hear the case. This prompted their replacement by three associate judges of the same Division who had to rule on the authors' appeals of the order to stand trial. Thus formed, the Division issued a ruling that amended the order to stand trial dated May 12, 2009 and determined that the authors should not be tried for peculation but instead for the offenses charged in the formal accusation. The Chief Justice of the Court suspended the associate judges at his own initiative because he considered their conduct irregular, and the State appealed the ruling issued by them. In order to rule on the appeal, three temporary associate judges were named to comprise the Criminal Division, based on the Court's January 21, 2009 ruling that allows the Chief Justice of the Court to appoint temporary associate judges when neither the regular judges nor the permanent associate judges can act. Thus comprised, the Division overturned the decision by the permanent associate judges on the classification of the offense, deeming that they had amended the decision by the regular judges at their own initiative without having the power to do so, since regardless of the Court's makeup it was the same jurisdictional body and, therefore, it could not overturn its own decision.

7.8 The Committee notes that the competence of the Criminal Division to rule on matters concerning the order to stand trial is not in dispute. The fact that its composition was altered on two occasions based on procedural rules does not affect the principle of the natural judge in the circumstances of the case, since said composition was determined pursuant to the laws in force, including the regular provisions governing the functioning of the Court, as asserted by the State party. Since the Committee does not constitute a fourth instance, it is not up to it to analyze the substantive content of the decisions adopted by the intervening judges.

7.9 The Committee hereby notes the statements of the President of the Republic asking for the removal of the associate judges; that on January 26, 2010, the National Assembly issued a resolution rejecting the associate judges' decision and requesting that their actions be investigated; and that the associate judges were removed and tried by the National Court for perversion of justice, although the case was ultimately dismissed.

7.10 The Committee hereby notes that the facts that led to the processing of the authors had profound repercussions on the economic and financial situation of the country, the consequences of which continued over time. The Committee takes note that within this framework the country's highest authorities expressed themselves publicly and made statements calling for those responsible for those events, persons who had headed up the country's most representative banking institutions, to be subjected to criminal penalties. This does not imply however that the manner in which the criminal proceeding was carried out against the authors and the final result of the investigation were due to, or were the consequence of, those public statements by representatives of the executive and legislative branches, or that such statements should have constituted a violation of any provision of the Covenant.

7.11 In light of the foregoing, the Committee deems that the facts set forth do not allow it to find for the existence of a violation of Article 14(1) and (2) of the Covenant.

7.12 With respect to the authors' complaint regarding the delay in the criminal proceeding, the Committee notes and agrees with the State party that the facts under judicial investigation were extremely complex from a substantive standpoint and due to the number of people involved in them. In addition, there were a great number of procedural motions and appeals that the Court was called to rule on. Taking these factors into consideration, the Committee does not have enough elements to allow it to find for the existence of undue delays, under Article 14(3c) of the Covenant, by the National Court.

7.13 The authors state that they were subject to violation of Article 15 of the Covenant since they were convicted in keeping with a criminal classification, bank peculation, provided for in Article 257 of the Criminal Code, which did not cover the facts charged, and that for this the courts made interpreted said article incorrectly. In addition, they were charged with conduct that dovetailed with the legal definition of "misuse," even though misuse of public or private funds as a form of peculation was decriminalized in 2001. The Committee notes that the issues related to the criminal classification applicable to the authors and the interpretation of Article 257 of the Criminal Code were subject to multiple procedural motions and rulings by different instances of the National Court from the start of the proceeding until the issuance of the cassation judgment, in which the evolution of the criminal classifications applied to the case was analyzed, including the nomenclature of bank peculation. Prior to the first instance conviction, the Criminal Division of the National Court ruled on the classification of the facts charged as peculation in three different compositions (regular judges, permanent associate judges and temporary associate judges). Moreover, the legal dispute surrounding the classification of the facts charged as peculation was what prompted the Division's regular judges to recuse themselves from continuing to hear it, the permanent associate judges to be removed and for a panel of temporary associate judges to be named. The same issue was also examined on appeal and on cassation. The authors' complaints before the Committee under Article 14(1) and (2) of the Covenant are also based on the dispute over whether the facts charged can be classified or not within the definition of peculation contained in Article 247 of the Criminal Code. The complaints under Article

14(1) and (2) and those concerning Article 15 of the Covenant are thus closely related. However, the Committee does not have the competence to elucidate the debate on the *ius puniendi*, or on the different criminal nomenclatures and their content, since it does not constitute a fourth instance.

7.14 The Committee recalls its case law according to which it is up to the courts of the States parties to evaluate the facts and the evidence in each particular case, or the application of the domestic law, unless it is demonstrated that such evaluation or application was clearly arbitrary or was tantamount to manifest error or denial of justice. The Committee notes that, according to the judgment on cassation, the conduct ascribed to the authors was already classified in Article 257 of the Criminal Code in force at the time the facts (bank peculation) occurred and that the amendment of 1999, subsequent to these, simply clarified what was previously established in relation to the active parties of the criminal classification. The Committee deems that there are not enough elements to assert that the interpretation of Article 257 of the Criminal Code made by the domestic courts was manifestly erroneous or arbitrary. Consequently, the facts described do not allow the Committee to find that there was a violation of Article 15 of the Covenant.

8. The Human Rights Committee, acting by virtue of Article 5(4) of the Optional Protocol to the International Covenant on Civil and Political Rights, is of the view that the State party violated the authors' right under Article 14(1) of the Covenant to a proceeding with due guarantees in the determination of their civil rights or obligations.

9. In accordance with Article 2, paragraph 3 a), of the Covenant, the State party is obligated to provide the authors with an effective remedy. In fulfillment of this obligation, the State must provide full reparation to persons whose rights recognized in the Covenant have been violated. Consequently, the State party must ensure that the pertinent civil proceedings comply with the guarantees in accordance with Article 14(1) of the Covenant and this Opinion.

10. Due its having become a party to the Optional Protocol, the State party has recognized the Committee's competence to determine whether or not there has been a violation of the Covenant. In accordance with Article 2 of the Covenant, the State party has agreed to guarantee all individuals within its territory or subject to its jurisdiction the rights recognized in the Covenant and to provide an effective and legally enforceable remedy when a violation is corroborated. Consequently, the Committee asks the State party so that, within a period of 180 days, it may provide information on the measures that it has adopted to apply this Opinion. The State party is also asked to publish the Committee's resolution and to broadly disseminate it in the State party.

Appendix

INDIVIDUAL OPINION (PARTLY DISSENTING) BY YUVAL SHANY, COMMITTEE MEMBER

[Original: English]

1. I agree with the Committee that Resolution AGD-UIO-GG-2008-12, approved by the Deposit Guarantee Agency dated July 8, 2008, together with Legislative Decree No. 13, approved by the Constituent Assembly the next day, violated the right granted to the authors in Article 14, paragraph 1, of the Covenant to be heard publicly and with the due guarantees by a competent court in order to determine their legal rights and obligations which, in this case, are their rights and obligations as individuals who suffered a confiscation of their assets in their capacity as directors and shareholders of Filanbanco. The Committee was also on target in dismissing the State party's objection *ratione personae*, alluding to the objective of the challenged measures to seize corporate assets, given that such measures encompassed the authors' private property, and they were deprived, as individuals, of the capacity to object to the lawfulness of such measures.

2. However, I not as convinced by the manner in which the Committee has considered the statement by the President of Ecuador asking for the associate judges to be removed and investigated, or of the manner in which it has considered the authors' assertions insofar as the retroactive application of Law No. 99-26, of May 13, 1999. Insofar as the President's statement, I do not agree with the Committee's position that the key issue is determining whether or not the "manner in which the criminal proceeding was carried out against the authors and the final result of the investigation were due to or were the consequence of those statements" (paragraph 7.10). The fact that a high ranking member of the executive branch asks for judges to be investigated and for them to be removed due to a provisional decision that they issued during complex criminal proceedings constitutes a serious act of direct interference with the independence with which

such proceedings are carried out. It is worth recalling in this regard that the right to be tried before an independent court is an absolute right*, in the sense that not only is it not subject to exceptions, but also that the right is not subject to the possible result of irregular proceedings. In other words, the right to be tried before an independent court can be violated even if it is not demonstrated that the result of the case was affected by the lack of independence. Consequently, I am of the opinion that the President's statement violated the authors' right to be tried before a court that is truly independent and that reasonably appears to be independent**.

3. With regard to the issue of retroactivity, the Committee correctly notes that it is generally up to the domestic courts of the States parties to evaluate the manner in which domestic law is applied. Nevertheless, under the circumstances of the present case, in which the Prosecutor General and the associate judges were of the opinion that the formal accusation should not contain the new offense of bank peculation due to the non-retroactive application of its new definitions, and given the above-mentioned interference by the executive branch in criminal proceedings, I continue to have doubts about whether the domestic courts' final position on the matter could be fully admitted by the Committee.

---

*. See Committee General Comment No. 32, paragraph 19.

**. *Findlay v. UK*, judgment of the European Court on Human Rights of February 25, 1997, paragraph 73.

Explanation of the Opinion of the U.N. Human Rights Committee in the Case of Communication No. 2244/2013 from the Brothers Roberto and William Isaías Dassum and Enforcement Thereof

Why did the state of Ecuador sign and ratify the International Covenant on Civil and Political Rights within the framework of the United Nations Organization (U.N.), together with more than one hundred and fifty states?

The main reason was to join in the planet's resolve to overcome aggression against the fundamental rights of individuals and have a suitable instrument to enforce respect for the dignity of human beings vis-à-vis the public power usurped by dictatorships and autocratic governments. It is an acknowledgment of the fundamental rights to freedom that ensure a life of dignity for all.

Why did the State of Ecuador sign and ratify the Optional Protocol (OP) to the U.N.'s International Covenant on Civil and Political Rights?

The reason was the need to acknowledge the right of private individuals to file reports (communications) against violations of rights recognized under the Pact and enjoyed by them, perpetrated by Member States (the State Parties), as well as the ability of the U.N. Human Rights Committee to declare the violation of international norms that recognize those rights, to order appropriate reparation, and to establish the procedure that must be followed therefor.

Who make up the U.N. Human Rights Committee?

The Committee consists of eighteen high-level specialists, selected on the basis of their cultural background and their expertise in the field of human rights. In the case of the Isaías brothers, these legal specialists came from the United Kingdom, the United States, Italy, Israel, Costa Rica, Argentina, Germany, and other countries.

DID THE BROTHERS ROBERTO AND WILLIAM ISAÍAS FILE THE REQUISITE REPORT OF THE VIOLATIONS OF THEIR RIGHTS UNDER THE COVENANT THROUGH ACTS COMMITTED BY THE GOVERNMENT OF ECUADOR?

Indeed. On March 12, 2012, the Isaías brothers filed the appropriate communication with the Committee. It was served on the State of Ecuador on June 5, 2013, and initially answered by the State Party on December 4, 2013, and subsequently on December 10, 2015.

IS THE DECISION IN THE OPINION OF THE U.N. HUMAN RIGHTS COMMITTEE BINDING UPON, I.E., MANDATORY FOR, THE PARTIES INVOLVED IN THE LITIGATION?

From the moment Ecuador became a party to the Optional Protocol, the State recognized the Committee's competence to determine whether a violation of the International Covenant on Civil and Political Rights had occurred and, therefore, the Committee's ability to sanction it, if a violation did indeed occur.

WHAT WAS THE "MATTER" THE U.N. HUMAN RIGHTS COMMITTEE HEARD AND DECIDED?

In the Isaías case, the Committee determined that the subject of the matter to be considered and decided was:

1. Criminal conviction; and

2. Seizure of property owned by the Isaías brothers.

WHAT DECISIONS WERE ADOPTED IN CONNECTION WITH THE "SEIZURE OF PROPERTY OWNED BY THE ISAÍAS BROTHERS"?

Two decisions were adopted by the Committee:

I. 7.4In the present case, the Committee Considers that the issuance of Constitutional Mandate No. 13, which expressly forbade the filing of actions for the protection of constitutional rights or others of a special nature against the actions of the AGD and included the instruction to remove from the bench, without prejudice of any potential criminal liability, any judges who would hear this type of actions, violated the authors' right, under Article 14(1) of the Covenant, to a process with due guarantees for the determination of their rights or obligations of a civil nature.

II. 8. The Human Rights Committee, acting under the provisions of Article 5(4) of the Optional Protocol to the International Covenant on Civil and Political Rights rules that the State party violated the authors' rights under Article 14(1) of the Covenant to a process with due guarantees for the determination of their rights or obligations of a civil nature.

WHAT RIGHTS ARE INCLUDED IN ARTICLE 14(1) OF THE ICCPR?

The human rights contemplated in the provisions of Article 14.1 of the Covenant are three: effective protection of the courts (Article 75, Constitution of the Republic of Ecuador [CRE]); due adjective process (Article 76, paragraphs 2 to 7, CRE); and due substantive process (Article 76.1, CRE).

> Article 14. 1. All persons shall be equal before the courts and tribunals. In the determination of any criminal charge against him, or of his rights and obligations in a suit at law, everyone shall be entitled to a fair and public hearing by a competent, independent and impartial tribunal established by law. The press and the public may be excluded from all or part of a trial for reasons of morals, public order (ordre public) or national security in a democratic society, or when the interest of the private lives of the parties so requires, or to the extent strictly necessary in the opinion of the court in special circumstances where publicity would prejudice the interests of justice; but any judgment rendered in a criminal case or in a suit at law shall be made public except where the interest of juvenile persons otherwise requires or the proceedings concern matrimonial disputes or the guardianship of children.

WHAT ACTS FALL WITHIN THE SCOPE OF BOTH DECISIONS BY THE COMMITTEE?

It is clear in light of its literal statement in paragraph 7.4 of the Opinion that the Committee declares that the act known as Constitutional Mandate No. 13 constitutes a violation of the right recognized in Article 14.1 of the Covenant: "In the determination of any criminal charge against him, or of his rights and obligations in a suit at law, everyone shall be entitled to a fair and public hearing by a competent, independent and impartial tribunal established by law," i.e., the right to the effective protection of the courts recognized in Article 75 of our Constitution. Mandate 13 barred access to jurisdiction and to a hearing conducted by a "compctent, independent and impartial tribunal established by law."

Moreover, it is clear that in paragraph 8 of the Opinion the Committee declares that the administrative act contained in Resolution AGD-UIO-GG-2088-12, approved by the Deposits Guarantee Agency on July 8, 2008, violates the right recognized in Article 14.1 of the Covenant: "In the determination of any criminal charge against him, or of his rights and obligations in a suit at law, everyone shall be entitled to a fair and public hearing by a competent, independent and impartial tribunal established by law," with reference to the right to due substantive process (due process of law) in administrative matters, a right recognized in Article 76, paragraph 1, of our Constitution.

This is what was stated in his individual opinion by one of the members of the Committee who participated in its deliberations over a four-year period. Not only did he vote in favor of the Opinion but wrote an enhanced concurring opinion in favor of the complainants. We transcribe below this opinion the Ecuadorian Ministry of Justice refuses to publish in its webpage:

Partial dissent by Committee Member Yuval Shany

1. I agree with the Committee that Resolution AGD-UIO-GG-2008-12, approved by the Deposits Guarantee Agency on July 8, 2008, together with Legislative Decree No. 13, approved by the Constituent Assembly on the following day, vi-

olated the authors' right, recognized in Article 14, paragraph 1, of the Covenant, to be publicly heard, with due guarantees, by a competent court in order to determine their legal rights and obligations which, in this case, are their rights and obligations as private individuals who sustained the seizure of their assets in their capacity as directors and stockholders of Filanbanco. The Committee also acted correctly in overruling the State party's ratione personæ objection, making reference to the objective of the challenged measures of expropriating corporate assets, inasmuch as the authors' private property was comprised within said measures and they were deprived, as private individuals, of the ability to oppose the lawfulness of such measures.

2. However, I am not as convinced by the manner in which the Committee has considered the declaration of the President of Ecuador asking that the associate justices be investigated and removed, nor by the way in which it has considered the authors' assertions with respect to the retroactive application of Law No. 99-26 of May 13, 1999. As regards the president's declaration, I do not agree with the Committee's position that the key question is to determine whether or not it has been shown that that the "manner in which the criminal proceedings against the authors unfolded or the final outcome of the investigation was influenced by the public statements made by representatives of the executive and the legislative branches or were the result of such statements" (par. 7.10). The fact that a high ranking member of the executive branch should ask that judges be investigated and removed by reason of the provisional decision they handed down in the course of complex criminal proceedings is a grave and direct act of interference with the independence with which such proceedings are conducted. It should be recalled in this regard that the right to be tried by an independent court is an absolute right in the sense not only that it is not subject to exceptions but also in the sense that said right is not subject to the eventual result of irregular acts. Or to put it differently: the right to be tried by an independent court may be violated even if it is not shown

that the outcome of the process was affected by the lack of independence. Therefore, it is my opinion that the president's statement violated the authors' rights to be tried by a truly independent court that reasonably appears to be independent.

3. With respect to the issue of retroactivity, the Committee rightly points out that it is generally incumbent upon the national courts of State parties to evaluate the manner in which national law is applied. This notwithstanding, in the circumstances of the present case, where the Attorney General and the associate justices opined that the complaint should not include the new crime of bank peculation because of the non-retroactive application of its new definitions, and considering the aforementioned interference by the executive branch in the criminal proceedings, I continue to harbor doubts as to whether the final position of the national courts in the matter could be fully admitted by the Committee.

WHAT WERE THE FACTS COMPLAINED OF IN THE COMMUNICATION AND DECIDED BY THE COMMITTEE IN DECISIONS I AND II TRANSCRIBED ABOVE?

The Opinion reads:

The facts according to the authors

[...]

2.16 Simultaneously with the criminal proceedings, AGD conducted civil seizure proceedings against the former shareholders and former administrators of Filanbanco, with the alleged purpose of securing payment of the debt with bank depositors at the time the institution was intervened. The proceedings began with Resolution AGD-UIO-GG-2008-12 of July 8, 2008, which provided the seizure of all the property of those who had been administrators and shareholders of Filanbanco until December 2, 1998. On this basis, and with no previous or administrative proceedings and with the support of law enforcement, the seizure began of more than 200 companies and other assets owned by the authors and other members of the Isaías group*. Furthermore, on July 9, 2008, the Constituent Assembly elected within the framework of the political process led by the President of the Republic, issued Constituent Mandate No. 13 to which it assigned constitutional ranking. This mandate ratified the legal validity of the aforementioned Resolution; declared that the Resolution could not be the subject of any actions for the protection of constitutional rights or any other special actions; and ordered that all actions filed be dismissed without the possibility of suspending or preventing compliance with the Resolution. Judges hearing any type of constitutional action related to that resolution and any actions taken to execute said constitutional action were to dismiss them under pain of removal from the bench and without prejudice of any potential criminal liability they may thereby incur. The Mandate further established that it was not "subject to any complaints, challenges, actions for the protection of constitutional rights, lawsuits, claims, opinions or administrative or judicial pronouncements."

2.17 The background to Constitutional Mandate No. 13 is Constitutional Mandate No. 1 of November 9, 2007, which prohibits controlling or challenging decisions by the Constituent Assembly. This Mandate establishes that judges and courts processing any action contrary to those decisions shall be removed and prosecuted. On June 10, 2010, Roberto Isaías Dassum filed an action seeking to declare Mandate No. 13 unconstitutional; it was dismissed on June 21, 2012, on the grounds of the immunity enjoyed by the Mandate.

2.18 The authors' appeals from this Resolution as well as from others which followed it for the purpose of expropriating property were to no avail. The Resolution stated that all the property of the authors, including property not intended for the operation of Filanbanco or any other company of that financial group, was subject to seizure, i.e., it included property intended for the authors' own personal use. In addition, sei-

---

*. The case file contains a list of the companies and other properties expropriated.

zure included properties which, according to public knowledge, were held to belong to the authors, i.e., independently of the ownership set forth in the respective property deeds.

The report

3.12 The seizure process likewise violated the right to due process. AGD is an administrative organ that may not evade the reach of Article 14 of the Covenant when it acts to determine rights and obligations of a civil nature. Taking this into account, the lack of an adversarial administrative procedure before AGD where the authors may exercise their right to a defense in advance of AGD's decision to expropriate their property violated the due process guarantees in Article 14(1) and (2) of the Covenant. The State availed itself of Mandate No. 13 to cloak the legal weakness of resolution AGD-UIO-GG-2008-12 with the ironclad mantle of jurisdictional immunity. Such immunity entails a violation of the right of access to justice, to due process, and to equal standing before the law and the courts in order to enforce rights of a civil nature, particularly the authors' property rights as former owners and shareholders of Filanbanco. Mandate No. 13 also violates the right to due process as related to Article 2, paragraphs 1 and 3 of the Covenant, by failing to respect the right to file an effective appeal and the authors' right to equal standing before the law. For the same reason, the Resolution and Mandate No. 13, taken as a whole, violated the right to equal standing before the law and to non-discrimination contemplated in Article 26 of the Covenant by denying specific individuals access to justice in order to assert their rights*."

WHAT IS ECUADOR ORDERED TO DO BY THE COMMITTEE?

9. In accordance with Article 2, paragraph 3), of the Covenant, the State party has the obligation to provide the authors

---

*. The authors state that a complaint against the Resolution, filed on June 28, 2010, was dismissed by the Provincial Court of Justice of Guayaquil under Mandate No. 13.

an effective remedy. In compliance with this obligation, the State must make full reparation to the individuals whose rights acknowledged in the Covenant may have been violated. Consequently, the State party must ensure that the pertinent civil proceedings are carried out with guarantees, in accordance with Article 14(1) of the Covenant and the present opinion.

10. By becoming a party to the Optional Protocol, the State party has acknowledged the Committee's competence to determine whether or not there has been a violation of the Covenant. Pursuant to Article 2 of the Covenant, the State party has undertaken to guarantee all individuals within its territory or subject to its jurisdiction the rights recognized in the Covenant, **and to provide an effective and legally enforceable remedy whenever a violation is proven.** Therefore, the Committee asks the State party to file, within a term of 180 days, information on the measures it may have adopted in order to apply the present opinion. The State party is likewise asked to publish the Committee's opinion and to afford it wide dissemination within the State party.

WHAT IS THE "EFFECTIVE REMEDY" TO BE EXERCISED ONCE THE VIOLATION OF DUE PROCESS HAS BEEN ASCERTAINED IN THE DECISIONS ON THE SEIZURES AND THE ISSUANCE OF CONSTITUENT MANDATE NO. 13?

With respect to the legal acts of a normative (Constituent Mandate No. 13) and an executive (the AGD seizure resolutions) nature the lack of validity of which has been declared by the Committee, both lack juridical efficacy ab initio. As decided in paragraphs 9 and 10 of the Opinion, "the State party has the obligation to provide the authors an effective and legally enforceable remedy ... whenever a violation is proven." Paragraph 9 states that in "compliance with this obligation, the State must make full reparation to the individuals whose rights acknowledged in the Covenant may have been violated."

The "effective remedy" the State must provide has to be suitable for the purpose sought, namely "full reparation" to the victims whose rights were violated. Of course, the "effective remedy" must be contemplated in national law and be appropriate for the reparation that must be made. Ecuador has contemplated that remedy in Article 16 of the Organic Law on Financial Administration and Control (LOAFYC) which contemplates the execution of the declaration of violation of rights mandatorily construed, as the Constitutional Court has done exercising the competence assigned to it by Article 436 CRE in Opinion No. 004-13-SAN-CC, published in the Second Supplement to Registro Oficial 22 of June 25, 2013 (4. "Said procedure consists of an execution proceeding in which the declaration of violation of rights shall not be open to discussion.") Therefore, the claim for full reparation to the Isaías brothers, which includes the petition for restitution of property and financial compensation (indemnification) must be made by way of a complaint in execution proceedings.

Both institutions, "effective remedy" and "full reparation," are defined in Resolution 60/147 on Basic Principles and Guidelines on the Right to a Remedy and Reparation for Victims of Gross Violations of International Human Rights Law and Serious Violations of International Humanitarian Law, issued by the United Nations General Assembly, approved on December 16, 2005; and published on March 21, 2006, Section VII, paragraph 10, and Section IX, paragraphs 17 to 20.

VII. Victims' right to remedies

11. Remedies for gross violations of international human rights law and serious violations of international humanitarian law include the victim's right to the following as provided for under international law:

(a) Equal and effective access to justice;

(b) Adequate, effective and prompt reparation for harm suffered;

(c) Access to relevant information concerning violations and reparation mechanisms.

IX. Reparation for harm suffered

15. Adequate, effective and prompt reparation is intended to promote justice by redressing gross violations of international human rights law or serious violations of international humanitarian law. Reparation should be proportional to the gravity of the violations and the harm suffered. In accordance with its domestic laws and international legal obligations, a State shall provide reparation to victims for acts or omissions which can be attributed to the State and constitute gross violations of international human rights law or serious violations of international humanitarian law. In cases where a person, a legal person, or other entity is found liable for reparation to a victim, such party should provide reparation to the victim or compensate the State if the State has already provided reparation to the victim.

17. States shall, with respect to claims by victims, enforce domestic judgments for reparation against individuals or entities liable for the harm suffered and endeavor to enforce valid foreign legal judgements for reparation in accordance with domestic law and international legal obligations. To that end, States should provide under their domestic laws effective mechanisms for the enforcement of reparation judgments.

18. In accordance with domestic law and international law, and taking account of individual circumstances, victims of gross violations of international human rights law and serious violations of international humanitarian law should, as appropriate and proportional to the gravity of the violation and the circumstances of each case, be provided with full and effective reparation, as laid out in principles 19 to 23, which include the following forms: restitution, compensation, rehabilitation, satisfaction and guarantees of non-repetition.

"In accordance with internal law," LOGJYC contemplates the manner in which reparation is to be made to the victims of violations of human rights under Articles 18 and 10:

Article 18. **Full reparation.** In case of a declaration of violation of rights, full reparation shall be ordered for material and immaterial damages. Full reparation shall endeavor that the person or persons who are the holders of the violated right enjoy this right in the most appropriate form possible and that the situation existing prior to the violation be restored. Reparation may include, among other forms, the restitution of the right, financial compensation, rehabilitation, satisfaction, and guarantees of non-repetition of the acts, the duty to refer to the competent authorities for investigation and punishment, acknowledgment measures, public apologies, the provision of public services, health care.

Reparation for material damage shall include compensation for the loss or deterioration of the affected persons' income, the expenses incurred by reason of the acts, and consequences of a pecuniary nature having a causal relationship with the facts of the case. Reparation for immaterial damage shall include compensation through payment of an amount of money or the surrender of goods or services susceptible of monetary quantification, for the pain and suffering caused directly to the affected individual and to those close to him, the impairment of values highly significant for the persons, as well as the alteration, in non-pecuniary terms, of the living conditions of the affected individual or his family. Reparation shall be made in accordance with the type of violation, the circumstances of the case, the consequences of the acts, and their effect on the individual's life plan.

The reparation judgment or settlement agreement must expressly mention the individualized obligations, both affirmative and negative, of the subject of the judicial decision, as well as the circumstances of time, mode, and place under which such obligations must be performed, except for financial reparation, which must be processed in accordance with the provisions in the next article.

The holder or holders of the violated right must necessarily be heard in order to determine reparation, at the same hearing if possible. Should the female or male judge deem it convenient, a new hearing may be set to deal exclusively with the matter of reparation; such hearing must be held within the next eight days.

Article 19. Financial reparation. Whenever part of the reparation should, for whatever reason, imply the payment in money to the affected party or the holder of the violated right, the determination of the amount shall be the subject of summary verbal proceedings before the same female or male judge, if against a private party; or in administrative proceedings, if against the State. An appeal may be filed only in those cases allowed by law.

Notes:

In Opinion No. 004-13-SAN-CC published in the Second Supplement to Registro Oficial 22 of July 25, 2013, the Constitutional Court declares the substitutive unconstitutionality of the final phrase of Article 19 of the Organic Law on Jurisdictional Guarantees and Constitutional Monitoring referring to: "Appeals, motions to vacate, and all other appeals contemplated in the appropriate codes of procedure may be filed in these proceedings" by the phrase "An appeal may be filed only in those cases allowed by law."

WHAT HAS THE HUMAN RIGHTS COMMITTEE RESOLVED IN CONNECTION WITH THE CHARGES RELATED TO THE CRIMINAL CONVICTION?

7.6 The authors affirm that the criminal proceedings violated their rights under Article 14 to be tried by a competent, independent, and impartial court, established by law; to the presumption of innocence; and to be tried without undue delays. In this regard, the Committee observes that the National Court was designated as having competence by virtue of the special jurisdiction that some of the codefendants enjoyed **and on the basis of internal procedural norms the interpretation of which it is not incumbent upon the Committee to question.**

7.8 The Committee observes that the Criminal Division's competence to decide matters related to the order to initiate proceedings is not at issue. The fact that its composition was altered twice on the grounds of procedural norms does not affect the principle of the natural judge in the circumstances of the case, for the decision on such composition was accomplished under the laws in effect at the time, including the norms which regulate the operation of the Court, **according to the affirmations made by the State party. Since the Committee is not a fourth instance, it is not incumbent upon it to analyze the substantive contents of the decisions made by the intervening justices.**

7.13 The authors affirm having been the subject of a violation of Article 15 of the Covenant due to their having been convicted of a crime, bank peculation, contemplated in Article 257 of the Criminal Code, which did not cover the acts imputed to them and that, in order to convict them, the courts abused the interpretation of said article. Moreover, behaviors were imputed to them that fell within the legal definition of "misappropriation" even though the misappropriation of public or private funds as a form of peculation was decriminalized in 2001. The Committee observes that the issues related to the type of crime applicable to the authors and the construction of Article 257 of the Criminal Code were the subject of numerous procedural motions and pronouncements by different divisions of the National Court since the inception of the proceedings through the handing down of the decision on the motion to vacate, which reviewed the evolution of the types of crimes applied to the case, including the nomenclature of bank peculation. Prior to the conviction at the trial court level, the Criminal Division of the National Court, in three different manifestations (justices, permanent associate justices, and occasional associate judges), had issued opinions on the classification of the acts imputed to the authors as peculation. Indeed, the legal controversy over the classification of the imputed acts as peculation was what caused the Division's justices to excuse themselves from continuing to hear the matter; the permanent associate justices to be removed from the bench; and the appointment of a division comprised of occasional associate justices. The same issue was also reviewed at the appellate and cassation levels. The grievances brought by the authors before the Committee under Article 14(1) and (2) of the Covenant are likewise based on the controversy over whether the acts imputed to them might or might not be included within the definition of peculation contained in Article 257 of the Criminal Code. The complaints under Article 14(1) and (2) and those related to Article 15 of the Covenant are, therefore, intimately related. **However, the Committee lacks competence to decide the debate on the *ius puniendi* or over the different criminal nomenclatures and the contents thereof, as the Committee is not a fourth instance.**

7.14 The Committee recalls its jurisprudence under which it is incumbent upon the courts of State parties to weigh the facts and the evidence in each particular case, or the application of internal legislation, unless it should be demonstrated that such weighing or **application was clearly arbitrary or tantamount to a manifest error or to the denial of justice. The Committee observes that, in accordance with the cassation decision,** the behavior imputed to the authors was already contemplated in Article 257 of the Criminal Code in effect as the time the acts occurred (bank peculation) and that the 1999 amendment, which was adopted subsequently to said acts, simply clarified what had been previously established in relation to the active subjects of the aforementioned crime. The Committee considers that there are insufficient elements to affirm that the interpretation of Article 257 of the Criminal Code made by the internal courts was manifestly erroneous or arbitrary. Consequently, the facts described do not allow the Committee to conclude that there was a violation of Article 15 of the Covenant.

The Committee makes it clear that it does not intervene in "the application of domestic law," for that is incumbent upon the courts of each State unless it is established that the application of the law "was clearly arbitrary or tantamount to a manifest error or to the denial of justice," and that it is necessary to provide it with "sufficient elements to affirm that the interpretation of Article 257 of the Criminal Code made by the internal courts was manifestly erroneous or arbitrary"; this shall be done through the filing of an appeal for review in accordance with Article 658 of the Integral Organic Criminal Code (COIP).

WHAT CHARGES WERE THE SUBJECT OF THE REPORT AND OF THE COMMITTEE'S DECISION WITH RESPECT TO THE CRIMINAL CONVICTION?

Based on what is set forth in the previous paragraph, the charges in the Isaías brothers' report must be demonstrated through the filing of an appeal to review their conviction (Article 658 COIP, highlighting the arbitrary application of criminal law when judges found non-existing facts that provide the basis for said application.

The charges made in the report or communication were as follows:

> 2.15 According to the authors, the above cassation decision aggravates the violations to the Covenant as: (a) It violates the principle of legality by retroactively applying the crime of "misappropriation" as a modality of the crime of peculation, a type of crime that had been decriminalized; it retroactively applied a less favorable criminal law, as it considered them as active subjects of the crime of bank peculation which, at the time of the indictment, was applied to circumstances much more limited; applied the aggravating circumstance of acting as a "gang," which has been repealed by the present Integral Organic Criminal Code; and applied the crime of peculation, which is indeterminate and precludes the defendant's defense; (b) It violates the principle of formal equality by applying more onerous sanctions than those which would have been levied in cases with identical facts; (c) It violates the principle of non reformatio in peius by imposing sanctions more onerous and crimes different from those contained in the appellate decision, thereby violating the right to a defense; (d) It violates their right to be tried by independent judges, as the justices who ruled on the motion to vacate had been involved in previous decisions in the same cause or had publicly evinced partiality.

www.ingramcontent.com/pod-product-compliance
Lightning Source LLC
Chambersburg PA
CBHW070407190526
45169CB00003B/1149